DOVES
FOR THE
SEVENTIES

poems for those who choose to care

DOVES FOR THE SEVENTIES

poems for those who choose to care

Edited and introduced
by
PETER ROBINS

CORGI BOOKS
A DIVISION OF TRANSWORLD PUBLISHERS LTD
A NATIONAL GENERAL COMPANY

DOVES FOR THE SEVENTIES

A CORGI BOOK 552 08323 2

PRINTING HISTORY
Corgi Edition published 1969
Corgi Edition reprinted 1972

Acknowledgements: pages 135–36
Copyright notices: pages 137–139

This book is set in Bembo 11 pt.

Corgi Books are published by Transworld Publishers, Ltd.,
Cavendish House, 57/59 Uxbridge Road, Ealing,
London, W.5.

Made and printed in Great Britain by
Richard Clay (The Chaucer Press), Ltd., Bungay, Suffolk.

**NOTE: The Australian price appearing
on the back cover is the recommended
retail price.**

INTRODUCTION

Hello. I've chosen these poems—about a hundred—from something over five thousand. It was part of my bargain with Corgi Books that there should be a national advertising campaign in connection with this anthology. It was agreed that the theme—the struggle now/tomorrow/always for peaceful living—was too urgent to limit contributions to any one literary gang or Rent-A-Bard clique. Again, it seemed to me that any comprehensive idea of what poets in these islands are doing in this same struggle wouldn't best be gained by my groping along shelves of slim hard and soft published volumes.

I've placed the poems in four groups. Movements if you like. Seasons if you're not musical. First, you'll find work that examines our inheritance—mental and geographical—as we move to the 1970s. Next a winter section in which the omnipresent battle zone is surveyed: classroom, street, home. This leads to poems which glance at the prospect before us: the terrible but never hopeless spring of racial strife, nuclear menace, thought-conditioning; so on. Finally, the resolution: the vision—if that doesn't scare the overgenteel into the loo.

There's the theme then. It didn't start yesterday. The resonant voices of Owen and Sassoon still echo here and there. Who'd have it otherwise? An armistice revokes the licence to murder but not the delight in destruction. That's just one variation developed in different ways by different poets. The theme is paramount throughout the book. That's why you'll not necessarily find all the work by any one writer in sequence. His or her age by the way is laughably irrelevant when the song not the popsinger is vital. You'll find no poems that report just Vietnam or Grosvenor Square. Colour television can do this so much better. Of the hundreds of manuscripts I read that described once again our latest horrors, too few looked through the headlines and back to the causes in ourselves. Too often a poem consisted of sincerity plus a couple of images gleaned from a poster or documentary. Sincerity to adapt Edith Cavell is not enough. Nor is trendiness.

Of the poets whose work you'll be looking at/saying/singing/shouting, I've met very few; drunk with fewer; lived with none. Don't try to work out literary league tables from the number of poems representing any one contributor. Poems were chosen for their relevance to the theme alone. Perhaps my most tedious chore has been rejecting bundles from aspirants to our literary establishment. In general I thanked them for their sparkling autobiographical details (unfailingly appended) and regretted that their work was so dreary by comparison.

At the turn of the century students linked arms to chant choruses from Swinburne's work as they processed the streets of one of our provincial university cities. The impact of the Forster and Butler Education Acts has done something to change our student population. And our poems. I still hope you'll croon some of these in your shower/whisper a verse across the pillow/add a tune or improvise a dance. I'm offering you a flight of doves that won't be caged; won't coo for you in a manageable way. You'll have to chase them through the library window into a noisy world.

In general the poems are lyrical. They sing. They celebrate living and loving despite the obstinate fact of death. Incidentally they may in part answer one Sunday critic's more witless aside that lyric poets have a limited octave. Incidentally they may sound a few notes to distract from the intemperate brayings of yesterday's rebels who—having taken respectability's pledge—can't recant volubly enough. Really they're for you.

PETER ROBINS
Kennington, S.E.11.   June 1969

DOVES
FOR THE
SEVENTIES

ONE

DEFINITION
(*for Jean Campbell*)

What is war my lord?
War is empire

What is war general?
War is manhood

What is war teacher?
War is inevitable

What is war preacher?
War is unfortunate

What is war fellow?
War is escape

What is war kind employer?
War is profit

Sister what is war?
War is a telegram

Brother what is war?
War is my impotency

Father what is war?
War is my trembling hands

Mother what is war?
War is three undiscovered graves

LAURENCE COLLINSON

THE LOVER, ON RETURNING
FROM THE WARS

The girl I had the night before I left
told me I had a body like a tree:
a sapling gum, she said, her fingers deft
to tug and twitch the hairy bark of me.
My flesh was flushed just like that gum—the one
that stretched itself, she said, in her backyard—
the red and rust of smiling sweeps of sun,
and not by time, or man, or weather marred.
That was before the war they said was mine. . . .
and pocked my skin, and turned my tan to grey,
and lopped my twig of sex, and seared my spine,
and stifled manhood's song in one long day.
Stunted and frail, I joke each time I fall;
girls have nothing to say to me at all.

LAURENCE COLLINSON

THE LONG WAR

Less passionate the long war throws
its burning thorn about all men,
caught in one grief, we share one wound,
and cry one dialect of pain.

We have forgot who fired the house,
whose easy mischief spilt first blood,
under one raging roof we lie
the fault no longer understood.

But as our twisted arms embrace
the desert where our cities stood,
death's family likeness in each face
must show, at least, our brotherhood.

LAURIE LEE

I SAW A MAN WITH POPPIES

I saw a man with poppies
in his hair,
whose bones shone through

his clothes, hold up
an hourglass
in his skinless hand.

He watched the grains of silver
fill the glass; then took
the wreath of poppies

from his head
and gave it me.
The hourglass cracked,

I saw
his bones white-hot
my hands

a crimson red,
and ditches filled
with fly-blown

horses,
mud
and men.

MICHAEL JOHNSON

ANOTHER PLACE

'On a hill near Jerusalem an old man watches the planting of the Martyrs' Forest—memorial to the Jewish victims of Nazi Germany.' *Caption from a pictorial history of Israel.*

An old man silent
on a silent hillside
where six million grow
because six million died

under low skies
burdened with grief
dug their own grave
laid their own wreath

star upon yellow star
stare upon stare
only a bullet
to answer a prayer.

Six million trees
in six thousand rows.
Because six million died
Six million grow.

JEREMY ROBSON

GOING FOR A SONG

Nothing too recherché this afternoon.
The skull, Tenth Ideology.
Typically dictatorial (note the jaw).
But died oddly, natural causes it would seem.

Next, a torso, nigger-brown;
strategically preserved in jazz, alcohol.
Could have been a plantation ornament.
Not rare; especially in some places.

Third (one of a pair) a female breast,
for passround later, as desired.
Notched. I would suggest
a nursing mother's, disturbed at feed.

Last, a child's foot.
Gaudy perhaps.
But with the maker's mark in genuine napalm.
Unpriced. Modern, at a guess.

GEOFFREY HOLLOWAY

NOW WE SHALL MARCH THROUGH STREETS

When our days were young
The air was full of our glory—
The jets screaming our triumph,
The villagers fleeing in a thousand directions,
And our rockets tearing into their heels.
Well I can speak
Of the mastery of metal over flesh—
Salvoes, machine-gun streams
Leaving blood flowing freely
Even gaily, in the blood season
Of our manhood.
I can write of power,
And nerve tangles of pleasure and fear,
Tenseness and excitement,
The godliness of sky and speed
Suggesting honour and importance—
Yet when I remember; when I think
Of howling motors and hailing metal,
I can set down nothing of significance—
Only some political ramblings
Not worth recall.

PETER MARSHALL

LEFT IN THE DESERT

left in the desert
his sorrow cheers
the whorl of cloud,
and the ants bite,
and the birds cry.
the lost,
the lost carnival:
the captain,
shouting colours,
irradiates death;
the bright sun of his dying
breathing life into the sad animals.

TREVOR LAWRENCE

A PINT BEFORE CLOSING TIME

old man of drunken habits
taking cider in the alcove
narrating your military service
and tales of a marabout mistress
poor as an acorn
and redounding of death

BRUTON CONNORS

THE SOLDIERS

That Autumn the last leaf fell
Sometime while I wasn't looking

The last one
And I didn't even see it go

Like we don't see them go

At least not marching through
The streets with a swagger
And a brave song
Not in a skirl and swirl
Of splendid red anyway

Yet we know they do go
Still
Something like that leaf
While we are looking the other way.

PHILIP PADFIELD

FOR AN EX-FAR EAST PRISONER OF WAR

I am that man with helmet made of thorn
Who wandered naked in the desert place,
Wept, with the sweating sky, that I was born
And wore disaster in my winter face.

I am that man who asked no hate, nor pity.
I am that man, five-wounded, on the tree.
I am that man, walking his native city,
Hears his dead comrade cry, *Remember me!*

I am that man whose brow with blood was wet,
Returned, as Lazarus, from the dead to live.
I am that man, long-counselled to forget,
Facing a fearful victory, to forgive:

And seizing these two words, with the sharp sun
Beat them, like sword and ploughshare, into one.

CHARLES CAUSLEY

BRIEFING FOR TROPIC WAR

now let us continue with the anti-mite undershorts
cellular   look upon it as your friend there
being a great diversity of bugs where you are
going more particularly in dry grassy areas where
the deadly projectile-cicada can move with the
speed and force of a ·303 rifle-bullet right up
your jacksy and cause painful death or paralysis
what will make you no good for anything   now
the enemy against what you are fighting is in
particular wily and dangerous in his tactic
cigarettes what give off phosgene and curried
prawns containing fishhooks tipped with curare
will all be placed before you likewise women
what are truly dynamite and detonate by touch
explode into 48 reticulated grenade-sections
kill everybody in the building   when this
happens it's called a rough house so remember
to keep yourself intact for your wives and
sweethearts or some pretty friend

BRUTON CONNORS

THE DAY WAS A BRONZE HARP

the day was a bronze harp
with sun entangled in its strings
Together with the trees
it sang a strange and lowly song
and small winds
added their laughter.

we created a new world that day
away from all the evil and pain
of men's petulant storms.
We built a land of streams
and mountains safe for man
and animals.
We coloured the sky the blue of peace
and the land the warm brown of joy.
Water nourished the land
and life surged forth.

the evening was a lute
with the moon trapped in its darkness.
Together with the stars
it hummed a mournful tune
and angels shivered behind
the night's stark imaginings.

On steaming horses
they found us at last
and saw the beautiful world
—saw the good land and pure water
and the animals lying at peace
in our arms.

with their hands
tore it into small pieces
and cast them onto the wind

and they fluttered away
like tissue butterflies

TINA MORRIS

NOT MARCHING AWAY TO BE KILLED

Peace is the men not marching away to be killed.
I never saw my father marching away to be killed.
He was killed before I was born. But my mother
Always spoke of the men marching away to be killed.
Not 'marching to the war' or 'into action'
Or even 'marching to fight for this country'.
Although she was a soldier's daughter and a soldier's
Widow. 'Marching away to be killed'
Was the fundamental reality for her.

                                        For me

Peace is the man I love not
Marching away to be killed.

JEAN OVERTON FULLER

ALEXANDER THE GREAT

apropos of Alexander: he did things
the deed, and the sign by which it may be known
as in the erection of trophies on a battlefield
or the founding of cities

he saw his world
from the muscular back of Bucephalus
it was not less lovely for bearing his mark
in its burned villages and scattered princelings

yet while Alexander's face is on the coins
those little things holding huge distances together
it is not a man that is worshipped but Heracles the god
along the Araxes in Bactria and at Thebes

and long after the man himself has gone
when his hatred is only a murmuring on the wind
the signs will be shown the buried dead forgotten
and his memory consigned to its place in the record of
    demons

ROBERT CONRAD

STRATEGY

Wiser, no doubt, to think of war in terms
of shaded maps, observing with what ease
the black and strictly impersonal line ploughs
deeply, reaping a harvest of towns—the names,

if tongue can sheave them, yours to string upon
the day's objective talk; safer to count
the score in planes, without extravagant
recourse to actual costs in minds or men.

Yet, for all your fables, you cannot avert
the untenable moment of knowing. Tidy
on wind and spiralling height, the falcon already
prepares its tearing descent to your heart.

Since every combatant's wound is your wound, too;
for every death, life pins the crime on you.

HOWARD SERGEANT

ANGEL BOLEY

There was a wicked woman called Malady Festing
Who lived with her son-in-law, Hark Boley,
And her daughter Angel,
In a house on the high moorlands
Of the West Riding of Yorkshire
In the middle of the last century.

One day Angel
Overheard her mother, Malady, talking to Hark, her husband,
Hark, said Malady, it is time
To take another couple of children
Into our kitchen.
Hark laughed, for he too was wicked and he knew
For what purpose the little children
Were required.

But Angel, who was not happy and so
Lived out her life in a dream of absentmindedness,
In order not to be too much aware
Of her horrible relatives, and what it was
That happened every now and then
In the kitchen; and why the children who came
Were never seen again, this time
When she heard what her husband and mother said,
Came out of her absentmindedness and paid attention.
I know now, she said, and all the time I have known
What I did not want to know, that they kill all children
They lure to this house; and that is why, when I pass in the
   village,
The people look askance at me, and they whisper—
But not so that I cannot hear—
There goes the daughter of Mother Lure. And the stranger
   says:
Who is Mother Lure? And they answer: Mrs. Festing and
   they make the sign

That is to protect them from evil. Selfish wretches, said Angel,
They do not mind about the children, that evil is not kept
    from *them*.
Angel wandered into the woods and she said: No more
    children
Are going to be murdered, and before they are murdered,
    tormented
And corrupted; no more children are going to be the victims
Of Mother Lure and my husband, Hark. Dark was the look
    then
On Angel's face, and she said: I am the Angel of Death.

Mrs. Festing and Boley
Always left the cooking to Angel, they despised Angel but
    Angel
Could cook, and that they thought was all she was fit for,
To cook and keep house. And they realised
It was far from being to their disadvantage that Angel was,
As they thought, half-witted, and never knew
Or wanted to know, what was going on around her.

As soon as Angel
Said to herself: I am the Angel of Death
She became at once very practical and went out into the
    woods and fields
And gathered some A. Phalloides, commonly called the
    'white' or deadly
Amanita, a mushroom of high toxicity.
These poisonous fungi she put into a soup, and this soup she
    gave
To her husband, Hark, and her mother Malady, for supper,
    so that they died.
Angel then went to the police and said:
I have done evil, but I have saved many children.

The Judge said: Why did you not tell the police
That children were being destroyed? There was no proof, said
   Angel,
Because there were no bodies. I never could find out
What they did with the children after they had killed them.
So then the police searched hard, the wells, the rivers and the
   woodlands,
But never could they find out where
The children lay. Nor had the parents of the children
At any time done anything but weep. For they thought their
   children
Had been bewitched and done away with, and that
If they told their fears of Mother Lure and her wickedness
To the police, they would not believe them, and more children
   than ever
Would disappear.

From then onwards in the trial, Angel spoke
No word more, except to say: I am the Angel of Death.
So they put her in a lunatic asylum, and soon she died
Of an outbreak of typhoid fever. The people of the village
Now loved Angel, because she had delivered them from the
   fear
Of Mother Lure and Hark Boley (who they thought was her
   paramour,
Although officially the husband of Angel) and had saved their
Little children from being tormented and slain by these
   wicked people.
So they wrote on her tombstone: 'She did evil that good
Might come.' But the Vicar said it was better not to put this
   but
Just her name and age, which was sixteen.

So he had the words
The villagers had written taken off the tombstone. But the next day
The words were again on the tombstone; so again the Vicar had them
Removed. And this time a watch was set on the grave,
A police constable and the village sexton watched there that night.
And no man came again to write on the tombstone
The forbidden words. Yet when morning came, again the words were on the tombstone.
So the Vicar said: It is the hand of the Lord.

And now in that graveyard, at that grave's head beneath the yew trees,
Still stands today the tombstone of Angel, with the words writ on it:
'She did evil that good might come.' May God be merciful.

STEVIE SMITH

I TOO AM CAIN

It is my breath rekindles Belsen's fires—
my lungs are bellows for those monstrous pyres.

There is no need to sleuth out homicides
among the shadows of midsummer's day;
search constantly among the whole world's flags—
they hide no man more culpable than I.

Not obvious in robes or uniforms
nor crisply suited in some boardroom stands
the suave destroyer. That primaeval face
here—in my mirror—lustily contends.

When I repel one shy kiss with a sneer
or crush a dove to paper underfoot—
if I pull back my hand from proffered hand:
then I am he whose nutriment is hate.

Part of myself must die or reinspired
must aim to dominate. For my same breath
which might bear praise as easily commands
—with growing pleasure—greater works of death.

Can I not see now smouldering in my eyes
those embers from which Belsen's fires may rise?

PETER ROBINS

ONE FOR SORROW

One for sorrow
Weep with me
Man come borrow
My sympathy

One for sorrow
Bow your head
Cain's hand raised
And Abel dead

One for sorrow
Mourn alone
For children
In a battle zone

One for sorrow
Count me out
When you join
The victory shout

One for sorrow
Know the cost
Of the war
Both sides have lost.

PHILIP PADFIELD

WHITE CHRISTMAS

Once by a river I waited
Till snow came at dawn like a friend
And the wind from behind me stopped blowing
And the signs said it was South Bend.

And I picked up my bag and my feet
And crawled out of my tent of a tree
And the road was pure white to Chicago
And the only thing black there was me.

But whiteness can sure be deceiving
Like cherry trees back in D.C.,
Though I never look out for no trouble,
Most places it comes to me free.

Chicago no doubt is no better,
There's plenty are willing to fight,
But god just to live for a while
Where people forget they are white.

KEN WLASCHIN

BRAINS FOR HIRE

I went, expenses paid, to Stalin's Russia
and saw people's progress, which I recounted
in Oxford lectures and for the Left Book Club;
wrote socially conscious novels and burning
verse in Mayfair about Welsh mining valleys
from real conversations (my telephone bill
was prodigious) and recall good sales in Spain
and Sydney. That was my thirties period.

Brains for hire, brains for hire,
Hit the mood and find the buyer.

For a time I was undecided whether
to be a conchie in World War Two, but my
friends advised Intelligence, surmising—as
it turned out, rightly—this held material
for postwar thriller fiction. I was then switched
to Information and transformed the nation's
cuddly bears from Teddy to 'Uncle Joe', for
which I got the Royal Victorian (fourth class).

Brains for hire, brains for hire,
Hit the mood and find the buyer.

After the war I sang, converted, of the
Free World, and denounced the rank conformity
and cynicism of international
communism in literary journals,
flung across Europe, which I founded, managed
and edited myself with American
foundation money. Foes named the CIA,
were sued, apologised, settled out of court.

Brains for hire, brains for hire,
Hit the mood and find the buyer.

My novels caught the tone of sex, antiques and
violence at its zenith; my concrete verse was
read with electronic music, massed banjos
and a pneumatic drill on the BBC;
I cut out sections of the walls of well-known
West End toilets and proclaimed them as a new
art form which no one dared to challenge and were
sold to the New York Museum of Modern Art.

Brains for hire, brains for hire,
Hit the mood and find the buyer.

I shone with Franco's sunny Spain in tourist
brochures, and unearthed Saudi Arabia
as the world's most democratic country for
a sponsored supplement, covered the Queen to
Canada and the Pope to Fatima and
found both events equally moving, and hailed
tax evasion millionaires as national
philanthropists deserving a life peerage.

Brains for hire, brains for hire,
Hit the mood and find the buyer.

I was converted from Against to For the
Common Market, and from Canterbury to Rome,
when I moved up Fleet Street. I was careful to
read back numbers of the paper to find out
my views on the United Nations and the
Commonwealth, Nasser, Aden, the balance of
payments and devaluation. I sold my
volumes of Russell and praised South Vietnam.

Brains for hire, brains for hire,
Hit the mood and find the buyer.

I rescued the fallen cigarette market
by linking smoke with God, devised a whiter
than white campaign for the Nigerian High
Commissioner, was photographed in fireproof
pyjamas on a slumberland mattress with
a blonde reading the latest Kingsley Amis
for next week's *Sunday Times* colour supplement,
and coined the phrase, 'Take a trip to inner space'.

Brains for hire, brains for hire,
Hit the mood and find the buyer.

DAVID TRIBE

THE NIGHTINGALE IN HELL

At night I have
heard the rest-
less Greek bird in
exile, its small
brown nut of a
heart cracked in the
vice of possessive
love, hang in fire and
crystal a coda
upon the black
and listening midnight.
What, tiny spirit of the
trees and white rocks
and cascades of distant
Thessalonica, small soul
unvanquished over vast
seas and the inhospitable
mountains of Italy,
over the patterned leagues
of Europe and her hundred headed
skies, what
do I hear you
cry? I hear the
hiss of the breasted
harp as the needle
enters, the high
waterfalling roar as
American naptha falls
in fire like snow upon
the blistering shoulders
of seraphim somewhere over
Asia. I hear the solitary and
chryselephantine groan

of the dead Austrian Minotaur
as a tender beloved note
touches the ulcerous
drumskin. I hear the
enormous grief of the mole
in the dark corridors,
consuming only the dead,
consuming only the dirt and
ash of the dead, only
the clay, the trodden clay
of the dead Dead.
I hear the mute
swan on the long
summered reaches
of this leafy river here
in the eastern marshes,
I hear her in the
deathchanting voice of
this small midnight
nightingale, ah, all the hopeless mythological deathsongs
of the Trumpeter over
Europe and her shame.
And I hear, far off,
the small flying heart of
the forsaken god son
singing as it
wings a way into
the orgulous furnaces of
helios and the
eternal and burning cages
of the day.

GEORGE BARKER

TWO

INNOCENT'S SONG

Who's that knocking on the window,
Who's that standing at the door,
What are all those presents
Lying on the kitchen floor?

Who is the smiling stranger
With hair as white as gin,
What is he doing with the children
And who could have let him in?

Why has he rubies on his fingers,
A cold, cold crown on his head,
Why, when he caws his carol,
Does the salty snow run red?

Why does he ferry my fireside
As a spider on a thread,
His fingers made of fuses
And his tongue of gingerbread?

Why does the world before him
Melt in a million suns,
Why do his yellow, yearning eyes
Burn like saffron buns?

Watch where he comes walking
Out of the Christmas flame,
Dancing, double-talking:

Herod is his name.

CHARLES CAUSLEY

INSTEAD OF A CAROL

No, not for us the plastic and the foil
Of decorations in symmetric coil
Decked out with vulgar art across the street
And shown to children for a festive treat.
Not sordid artificial christmas tree
With squalid tinsel where the leaves should be.
Not disenchanting santa in the store
With beery double in the shop next door.

Instead for us the exiled son of man,
New born in outhouse lying in the cold,
Though not for us one special holy boy
But everyone unwanted and unloved,
The lonely and the helpless and the poor,
The little hungry child in every land.

TOM EARLEY

WALLFLOWER YOUTH

The window lies open
on all summers

the Jewel beautiful
glistens: untouched,

the hand clasps
strong around the rock
in desire

kissing only the movements
of turbulent passions
in flight

standing in the bus queue
on the eve
of everything.

DEREK TELLING

THE NEXT VILLAGE WE TOOK

After we'd blunted our swords on their menfolk we all met up
round the back of the church. There was Eric the smith and
John's son and they'd caught themselves a good bit of prime
meat very nicely packaged.

We formed in queues to have her, more out of devilment than
desire, but she wouldn't play for some of the lads who'd
come in last—just lay crying in the grass.

Then Eric turned a bit hard and he clubbed her skull to bits
with his sword's hilt (and only one blow it took him).

Then he straightened her out and had her just like that. Her
bab was running round and shouting at us why his mother's
head was nasty and she wouldn't talk to him or anything.

Some of the lads laughed and got back in the queue to have
her again, but myself I didn't want to look because she'd
reminded me too much of my own wife.

GEOFF BARNBROOK

AN HOUR LATER HE
DIED

a Biafran nightmare

An hour later he died
the child of innocence
and during the hour
unconnected people talked
not of his death
but of its cause

the child of innocence
heard not the people
nor knew the cause
he knew he was hungry
and knowing
            he died. . . .

DAVID BLATCHFORD

THE LAST ONE

On Mondays the confused beasts
Would come, flapping down the lane
To the smell of doom, and terror caught
Plunge through the gate left gaping
Churn the neat garden up and in turn
Terrify my flying mother.

Then soundlessly we children would converge
In the afternoon on the slaughter house
To watch objectively as children can
The game between the bullock's wit
And the wielding pole axed men begin.

Engaged to strike the chosen beasts
On the vulnerable spot between the horns
Until the strongest last of all
In slavering frenzy slithered round
The cobbles steaming mire and dung.

So felled his country image fled.
Ugly the heap of spattered pride.
The men would tell us clear off now
And we, released by death, as they,
Would play some other game instead.

MADGE HALES

IN HIS FOOTSTEPS

Your pregnant womb
balloons with genesis.
You wonder what pain
must be laboured through
before the first attempts to cry
burst forth.

Now,
as you watch his thriving legs
run-and-jump through hopscotched days,
you remember the hospital,
full of first and last cries,
hygiene and hygiene-white walls.

One day he breaks the window
you watched him through,
and you remember fearing
someone would teach him destruction
start him on the path of his father
in the nightmare yard where he raped you.

    PAUL HART

GLASGOW SLUMS

Rats run, unheeding, through the court
or stop to drink
from scum-topped, stinking pools
that make the place a bog.

A dog rakes, mindless, in the waste
from dustbin dropped
and scatters as he goes
a swarm of buzzing flies.

And, overall, a smell, a stench
of damp, disease, decay.
The crumbling walls,
the perilous slates,
the shattered panes,
the filth, the muck.

And, in the midst of this
a child plays, heedless and content,
accepting
never questioning
that this is right, or kind, or just.

GEORGE HARDIE

THUG

School began it.
There he felt
the tongue's salt lash
raising its welt

on a child's heart.
Ten years ruled
by violence left him
thoroughly schooled,

nor did he fail
to understand
the blow of the
headmaster's hand.

That hand his hand
round the cosh curled.
What rules the classroom
rocks the world.

RAYMOND GARLICK

TEACHERS

A teacher without a cane,
Is like a soldier without a rifle;
But who is the enemy?

J. H. THOMAS

SEEN AGAIN

Greatly maligned, because half-deaf,
you were the school's star turn,
the cunning ace up every joker's sleeve,
the mention of your name enough to draw

firm applause from the ranks of sour
boys you tried to teach. How we lapped
the stories up! One especially, of you
lying drunk and mascara'd in Soho Square,

flushed with lechery. Absurd, but we
believed it all, pointing and chortling,
inventing the semen's stain.
We gave you a name I won't repeat

hounding you with barks and yelps
quite openly. And when finally
'Where's that noise?' you said, peering
left, we'd point the other way.

Tonight, spotting you after these years
in the station's light, the same quiet
wife on your arms, it all comes back:
along with horror, shame, regret,

but admiration also for a stoicism you,
as Classics master, might accept.
And with this flares a loathing for
those other, surer men, who swooped

to bring back order when you failed:
who mocked you too, and doubly so,
by innuendo, sneer, and more.
Those relics of the barrack square,

bemedalled, dressed for Corps, raising
their sticks and egos readily
and physically at the faintest call
to mould a new generation of Cain.

JEREMY ROBSON

NEWS OF A DISTANT WAR

I do not want to look
at the naked boy
under the letterbox.
I do not want to know.

I do not want this truth
brought home at breakfast:
the eyes like bowls
of exhausted charity,
the target in his chest,
the destitute bones.
I do not want to see his mouth
while I drink coffee.

I know that were he fed
like his country's guns,
fed in the teeth of hunger,
dressed to kill,
he would not sacrifice routine
but, unremarked, obey
the trigger of a word,
and would be beautiful.

He would not, then, smiling
detonate the news,
or ever beg the question,
overthrow my views.

JAMES CORBETT

CRAZY HORSE THE SIOUX

Crazy Horse was a Sioux,
so listen to this!
He fought the whites,
    (you know, Custer
    and all that).
Rosebud, Wolf Mountain,
and the Wagon Box,
he was at them all.
Finally, one day,
    Buffalo all gone,
    kids starving,
    young men dead,
he decided to seek a truce,
so he rode to the reservation.
    'Ok, Crazy Horse, welcome.
    Sure we'll talk peace, just
    step into this small, dark
    iron room.'
But Crazy Horse was no fool.
He was all Sioux
and he made a break.
Some reservation Indians
grabbed him
            and a soldier
bayoneted him in the guts.
Crazy Horse the Sioux
    should have stayed
    in the wilds.
It's safer.

JIM BURNS

KIND OF EXPENSIVE

'They told me about the sixty-five dollars a month additional
combat allowance. I was in Oakland, California, so bored you
know. I thought with that money I could get a tape-recorder
and so on but of course I didn't know what I was going to
buy·it with—naturally in this kind of place all that stuff
comes kind of expensive.'

U.S. Marine, quoted in newspaper report

They shipped me over there,
suitably equipped with a rifle,
uniform, helmet, everything
in fact, except a tape-recorder.

The first fight wasn't so bad,
I killed a man, though
in doing it I lost my helmet,
got hit in the head, tasted blood.

The second was a little worse.
We were trapped in a village,
my friends were all killed.
I was wounded again, and cursed.

And the third was when I died.
I stepped on a mine, it blew
off my leg. I heard such strange
music as I was drained of blood.

JIM BURNS

PIETÀ

She holds him to her
    her arm soft round
his shoulder, her hand
clutching a pitcher

as she tries to wash
    his scalp forehead
    eyebrow eyelid
and cheek where the flesh

melts. We are to blame.
He is still alive
    whose five years have
borne a cross of flame.

(*from SEVEN AGAINST VIETNAM*)

KEITH BOSLEY

SONG OF THE MAD SHOWMAN

Roll up! Roll up! For the greatest show
That never was seen on earth,
Where the conjuror's word is the rule of law,
Esteemed at its own true worth.

Roll up! For the fishes and the fine white loaves
That shall feed the hungry ones
While the elephant roams through the wild sugar-cane
And tells 'em to stuff their buns.

Bravo! Alley oop! For the sad white clowns
That tumble the wild beast show,
Through the elephant feet and the snarling jaws,
Their search is old as the jungle laws,
For the fragments of the magic stone
That the love-laws may be viable,
The beasts are trained to leave them alone
But nature is unreliable.

Walk up! Walk up! To the thin high wire
Where the acrobats cheat the grave,
The crocodile jaws are snapping wide
While the hawk hangs poised on the opposite side
And the cat is gathered for the final spring,
There's a terrible gravity in this thing—
The nets may fail to save.

Dive in! And greet the performing soul
With a garland of gold-fish roes,
Come fish—dive deep to the bottom of the sea,
To the bottom of the sea
Where the great whales be,
To the sand no footprint ever trod
Where the only eye is the eye of God,
And rise again to the brass-band strain
To balance the world on your nose.

Belt up, Mad Jack, silk hat and whip
In the circle of rape-bred strife,
For to my life's end I will pretend
As the dead march home to the fife,
I must and will return again
Return again?
Return again
To the awesome hush that the conjuror spread,
Water to wine in the marriage bed,
Dance of the cripple and the blind man's sight
When the dead men come to life.

PATRICIA DOUBELL

THE RUNAWAY HEART

Did you hear the story of Boss McGroo?
He was awful sick and they said he was through,
Then along came the men of the medical art
And they fixed him up with a plastic heart
Up and down up and down up and down—

And that old ticker was a stayer and a sticker
With a dogged old din like Rin-Tin-Tin,
With a postulating clangour of a spanner in the works,
It was givin' him the jiggers and the jeebees and the jerks,
It was givin' him insomnia day and night,
He could turn him left, he could turn him right,
Now ho down death for a sting-a-ling-ling
But 'twas 'gainst the law to stop the thing
Up and down up and down up and down—

Now McGroo was a man never tangled with the law,
The millions that he made were always making plenty more,
Well, some said five and some said seven,
But he'd made that money with good clean livin',
He bowed him low to the bald-headed eagle
And his word to the young men was 'Do it legal'
Up and down up and down up and down—

But he knowed of a man in Arkansaw,
He'd had some dealin's with him before,
He'd had occasion to use his gun,
Paid him well for a job well done,
That man could shoot like he'd give you a pill,
And the name of that man was Billy the Kill,
So he went to that man and said 'Billy be smart,
Put a bullet right through this goddam heart',
But 'Boss, you're crazy' Billy replied,
'I got my principles, got my pride,
An' I never shot at a crazy man,
There's things you can't do, an' things you can,

I never shot a man that wanted to die,
An' you didn't oughta ask that much of a guy'
Up and down up and down up and down—

Then McGroo said Billy was mean and cheap,
And he called him chicken and a pimp and a creep,
And he cussed him up into one big heap
And he wouldn't let him eat and he wouldn't let him sleep,
Last thing he said he'd double the figure
And Billy began to debate with his trigger,
And he sure was havin' some rough ride
Overcomin' his principles and his pride
Up and down up and down up and down—
He put his hand in his pocket at last,
And he heaved a sigh—he didn't draw fast,
But the gun in his hand shone black and glossy
When in walked the Sheriff with a six-man posse
Up and down up and down up and down—

'You kin shoot that man in Mexico
Or any place else you care to go,
You gotta live, you gotta kill,
I don't condone it but I guess you will,
You kin bury 'em deep under six foot o' turf,
But not in a town where I'm the Shurf'
Up and down up and down up and down—

Then McGroo lit out with one big yell
And what he did then would be hard to tell
For the hammer of the heart-beat rose and fell
Like a hammer on the clamour of the damned in Hell
And he hit the roof and he shook the ground
And he laughed and he hollered and he danced around
And he frit the life out of Billy and the boys,
'Twas the only way to drown the noise,
And the runaway heart went over the hill
McGroo! McGroo!

And the runaway heart went over the hill
And for all I know she's goin' still
Up and down up and down and the prairie tells
Of a millionaire said his fare ye wells
To the heart beat hammering of Hell's own bells,
Up and down up and down up and down up and down
Up and down up and down up and down—

PATRICIA DOUBELL

THE WHITE DOO

The Doo rose heich	(dove) (high)
Syne swooped doon	(then)
Tae the wuid o pines,	(wood)
Pines green an prickly;	
Pines taa an strocht.	(tall) (straight)

Whit a fine bird,
Says the man
Wi rifle i haun.   (with) (hand)

Aye, says I.
Sae white, an breist   (breast)
Roon; wing sae white.   (round)
Nae trace o grey.
White, pure white.

An the Doo rose frae the pines,
Circled again and again,
Weaving a pattern,
A sang tae ma lovin ee.   (eye)

Tae be free lik yon,   (like) (that)
Says I.
Free. Tae drift,
Rise an faa wi each whirl   (fall)
o win.   (wind)

Wad be fine stuffed,
Says the man
Wi rifle i haun.
I've never seen
Yin as perfect.

An sic a thocht;   (thought)
That man could destroy
Sic a bird;
Could destroy
That which is free
An lovely tae the ee,

Made me rant
Against this man's idiocy.

Destroy that bird,
Says I.
Whit kin o thocht is this.   (kind)

Wad ye murder   (would)
Fir the sake
o some stuffed ornament.

Wad ye mak o this White Doo,
A Reid Doo o death.   (red)

    Aye, says the man;
    An wi yin crack,   (one)
    The act wis done.

I raged at the man
As I hurried tae the pines.

    That Doo'll be fine stuffed.
    Man, whit dae ye care.
    It's jist a bird.   (just)

    God, ye mak me lauch.   (laugh)
    You an your fine ideas.
    It's jist a bird.

And in that wuid o pines,
Pines green an prickly;
Pines taa an strocht,

I found that White Doo,
A mess o reid-grey feathers.
A scattered mess o Man's doing.

The White Doo
Noo ugly   (now)
Tae whit wis
An should hae been.

DAVID MORRISON

HORSES IN A FIELD

still as mud
in the crows' shade.
whimperless:

the bloodshot squirming eye
unblinking at the settled fly,
and the rats' feet unheard,

lies the crushed horse

I saw him die
under heavy metalled hooves:
the powerful, veined cruel legs
of other horses,

who drink clear water now
and move, unmoved,
in twilight.

MICHAEL JOHNSON

POLITICAL PRISONER

as sweat breaks out

he stalks
angry flies
upon the window pane
with open match box,
slides the cover shut
and throws the buzzing
cargo in the air. . . .

his wet hair freezes

. . . opens a crack
to let the fly see light
and closes
on the clutching leg
till screamless struggles
tear it off. . . .

eyes sting salt

. . . now lets the head emerge
snaps shut,
and hears the creature crack,
sees yellow ooze
between its kicks. . . .

MICHAEL JOHNSON

COFFEE ON THE BALCONY

the haze rising off the wet morning
the first sunshine raining through
the wet green leaves
the balcony. . . .
               with coffee
or how it could be
listening to the singing
of the day
if it werent for the crossfire
of you shooting your wife
her shooting you

PETE HOIDA

MAGMATIC

Deep in the magma of plutonic minds
begins the violence that bombards air,
a sub-acute, pre-active rage that blinds
the levelled eye and shatters what is fair.
Such anger, born of fear, erupts to fight;
the loosely-swinging hand becomes a fist,
and flick-flash thrusts blood-stain the streets of night;
the arm of peace withdraws a severed wrist.
Erupted anger, hurling ash and stone,
cremates the landscape, actors and the act,
till rage withdraws to its magmatic zone,
and deeds lose truth and legend buries fact.
    Deep in the magma peace begins again,
    and men rebuild to nullify their pain.

MARGERY SMITH

ON SEEING VOSKHOD OVER EDINBURGH

On a cold October night
Edinburgh's sky was punctuated,
Not by a divine presence,
But by the stabbing cigarette-end-like apparition
Of three men in a spaceship.
I looked out from my house
In a hundred-year-old tenement
And felt that Komarov, Yegerov and Feoktistov
Were fellow travellers of mine.
For it's a long way from Zazakhstan to Scotland
And it's a long way my home is from Voskhod.
Yet I saw
The stabbing cigarette-end-like shape,
I watched as the red light flashed
Across the sky.
For four minutes we Scots saw
The scientific age in action.
And as we retreated back into our tenements
And thought once more of slums,
We also saw that an alternative exists.

ALAN BOLD

TRAMP IN A WELFARE STATE

Litterbin searches
punctuate
his daily miserytour.
His clothes are maps,
with boundary-stitches
not the work of woman.

Along your neatly-paved pathways
he is a drudging canvasser
for the party we should all support.

PAUL HART

CAPTAIN LEONARD FEATHER

Captain Leonard Feather of
the Bomb Disposal Squad
was an expert in ballistics and
he placed his trust in God.

He had a way with hand grenades
a style with ammunition
he knew ballistics backwards but
he had no way with women.

He gave his bombs the names of stars
    like 'Marilyn Monroe'
but frustration was his downfall and
    eagerness his foe.
In his dreams he could imagine himself
    Casanova-style
taking all the girls apart and making it
    Meanwhile. . . .
his long white fingers picked at bombs
    and took away their hearts
    but when it came to women he
        was left alone. . . .
            in parts.

PETE MORGAN

BALLAD

My mother she whispered to me of the sea
My father spoke loudly of gold
My brother he cried of adventures to be
My sister said you shall grow old.

My mother she dreamed of great oceans of blue
My father he bought and he sold
My brother he fled to a world that was new
Leaving sister and me in the old.

My mother she died on a waterless plain
My father in business I'm told
My brother he crashed among jungle cane
My sister and I we grew old.

Now I wonder what mother wanted with sea
And father he with his gold
I wish I could search for my brother so free
My sister says I am too old.

KEN WLASCHIN

THREE

THE DEATH OF THE NUCLEUS

Why do these leaves shrivel
Before the autumn winds have come?
Why are my feet and hands
Before winter numb?

Why those clouds
Outshadowing thunder with their bulging peaks?
That sudden noise so loud
The eardrum of humanity cracks?

Atoms of flesh and water
Have been split apart.
Man is bereft of matter,
His blood poisons his heart.

DAVID CRAIG

DEMOLITION

I thank the amoeba for
My stomach juice's wonderful flow;
The fish for my backbone;
The frog for lungs;
And all animals together
For my strong skeleton;
Last, the tree-foot apes,
And all simians,
For my lobed brain
And instrumental thumbs.

And I report to them
That we, their heirs,
May, with our bomb,
Destroy the fruit of millions of years,
Our children;
Ourselves, as well, of course,
And, incidentally, all them.

NORMAN ILES

A POEM FOR CHRISTOPHER

Do not speak to him of love,
The warm, guitar-note kisses of a night
Tangling the smoke and star-dust in confusion. . . .
   (*'I once have loved—swan rush of sudden music*
   In ragged autumn sunlight and steel skies. . . .'
But that was in another country
And the girl is dead.)

Do not speak to him of fear,
The cold leukaemia of a waning soul,
Hammering heart against the caging ribs. . . .
   (*'For I once knew wild panic in the blood,*
   All soul sang free, my hope blazed to the skies. . . .'
But that was in another country
And the cause is dead.)

Do not speak to him of life,
Petitions against universal death,
Cold respite won, however rash the price. . . .
   (*'I once dreamed peace, children and dusty cornfields,*
   Free singing to no alien-clouded skies. . . .'
But that was in another country
And the land is dead.)

Do not speak of seed and blood,
Doomed procreation, crossed and tangled limbs,
The future cradled in a crippled womb. . . .
   (*'The tanks came where the women stood in line*
   For bread—and sudden gunfire rocked the skies. . . .'
But that was in another country
And they all are dead.)

Do not speak to him of hope,
The triumph of just causes, wild acclaim,
New treaties signed, peace, pact or what you will. . . .
   (*I too once fought, I too once knew the fire*
    To claw reluctant freedom from the skies. . . .'
But that was in another country
And the heart is dead.)

    VERA RICH

EVENT

Do you dare believe
what my garden shows?
Nobody wants to.

Yet, some have seen
gulls make beaches
pebbly with their eggs,
and some have watched
grown turtles swim in sand
until they drown.

I heard, today,
why a neighbour's wife,
proud from hospital
with her firstborn son,
went mad: the child has
bitten off her breast.

And, in the North,
they say the barley
lacks its beard.

These may be
rumours, hot sensation,
merely gossip.
My garden, I confess,
bears no glass fruit;
cannot compete, not yet.

All I can show
is one wild white sparrow
made from dust.

JAMES CORBETT

MEDALS

Who now strike stars,
base medals for new war?

Who contemplate·
awards, who mock defeat?

Who, dreaming, pin
what victory to what chest?

Who buff their pride,
How, why, for whom?

Who suffer and who win?

JAMES CORBETT

GREENHOUSE

Line upon line of cuttings,
tangle of tendrils and foliage vibrant
with sap, lit here and there by
geranium flame.

Clusters of fern absorbing the
soil's wetness,
breathing out an earthy musk into
the warmed air.

Flower pots crowded into
glowing ranks stretch
away down the staging seemingly
for ever.

The greenhouse pulsates with life.
Populated with plants it is
the world in a bubble—
all we need.

We do not strain to
look beyond the transparent walls
nor remember that glass
is brittle.

We do not notice the
sky outside start to thicken,
turn to steel, descend as though
to crush us.

Are caught unawares by
the thunder's sharp explosion shivering
the fragile structure that
surrounds us.

A hail of silver bullets
strikes the pane above us.
We look up at last
and realise

how thinly screened we are;
how soon our shelter may be shattered,
our world splintered into
smithereens.

PAT ARROWSMITH

PRISON DRAWING
(Holloway, February 1969)

Evenly spaced ribs
curve upward to the
skylight:
bent wand trunks of a leaning avenue
meet overhead,
bone the thin vaulting
arched above us.

Look from the top storey
down the cage of an immense
lift shaft,
ringed regularly with landing upon landing
linked by metal lace of
stairways.

See through an inverted telescope the
distant ground floor—
atoms of a chess board,
minute tile pattern,
black square white square black square
set in rows.

Run your eye along the landings.
Deep set door after deep set door
neighbour one another at
equal intervals.
Corridors reach, taper towards a
many-paned cathedral window
flanked by two small replicas.

This whole structure
intricately strung together with a
pencil work of railings,
cobweb of safety net:
verticals, parallels, circles,
diamonds, adjacent triangles
trellised in a geometry repeated
at each level.

Down my sentence the days vary,
the weeks copy each other.
The strands of my stretch
interweave in complex harmony,
restful symmetry.
I am at peace.
I do not want to leave.

PAT ARROWSMITH

'YES,' I SAID, 'BUT IS IT ART?'

Took me to the battlefield
saw the mushroom cloud
said 'We can see the colours even
when our heads are bowed.'
Showed me the destruction
the slaughter a la carte
said 'Isn't Nature wonderful.'
'Yes,' I said
'but is it Art?'

Took me to the scientist
opened up a phial
said 'This is only chicken-pox
and rhino bile.'
Showed me what it did to mice
said 'That's just a start
but isn't Nature wonderful.'
'Yes,' I said
'but is it Art?'

Took me to the hospital
pulled aside the sheet
said 'Look at that pulsating
listen to the beat.'
Showed me the incision
threw away the heart
said 'Isn't Nature wonderful.'
'Yes,' I said
'but is it Art?'

Took me to the tenement
opened every door
said 'Have you seen the copulation
practised by the poor?
We select the ones to breed
and we reject a part
but isn't Nature wonderful.'
'Yes,' I said
'but is it Art?'

Took me to the prison
threw away the key
said 'If you learn our lesson
you could still be free.'
Pointed out the spy holes
and my adaptation chart
said 'Isn't Nature wonderful?'

   'Yes,' I said.

PETE MORGAN

THE PHOTOGRAPH

They photographed me young upon a tiger skin
And now I do not care at all for kith and kin,
For oh the tiger nature works within.

Parents of England, not in smug
Fashion fancy set on a rug
Of animal fur the darling you would hug.

For lately born is not too young
To scent the savage he sits upon,
And tiger-possessed abandon all things human.

STEVIE SMITH

THE THINKING ANIMAL

The cattle which smell the blood,
Of their slaughtered kin,
Bellow their protest, their will to live;
We, with Hiroshima in our nostrils,
And Nagasaki in our brains,
Can do no less.

J. H. THOMAS

MARTYR

Yellow-robed, on cathedral steps,
under the whine of jets, where tanks stalk,
the spit of Jesus, of any man,
with no shade but truth, I burn.

Burn for a thought, a stake in freedom,
speech between humans, a common loaf;
that roaring pride, this raging end,
your soul's asbestos, life.

Hear my black flesh. Begin.

GEOFFREY HOLLOWAY

PASSION 67

Is this carcase
your body, then?
this seething mass
of judas-men

your mystical body?
the mystery
behind the pain
of history—

behind the curias,
synods, boards,
sanhedrins, stakes,
torments and swords?

Into your heart
are thrust the spears
that persecute
two thousand years—

all in your name:
the holy war,
the forced conversion,
blood-red roar

of flame and crowd
and inquisitor's shout;
the silencing,
the roundabout

discreet undoing—
all have cried
anew Let him
be crucified.

Bishop-purple and
cardinal red
the weals and bruises
about your head.

Sleek as nails
the laws that cheat
the freedom of
your pinioned feet.

Neat as thorns,
Geneva bands
bind the healing
of your hands.

We, your body,
who crucify you,
unlike the soldiers
know what we do

as we speak our spears
and think our thorns,
and nail our brothers
up on the horns

of all the crosses
history knows,
lining time
in unending rows.

Catholic, protestant,
heretic, knave;
freethinker, deviate
sure to deprave;

anarchist, communist,
negro, jew—
we offer each of them
up to you

as a sacrifice,
and freely flood
your altars with
our brother's blood.

This is your body—
pharisees, scribes,
and sinners all:
that preacher's jibes

at Canterbury,
Geneva, Rome;
this prelate's pride,
that seeks to comb

the heart's ore out,
turn to a clod
the freedom of
the sons of God.

Still we rip
your robe apart
with every hook
of the human heart;

of mine as well—
the publican, thief,
whose deeds might be those
of unbelief,

so little they have
to do with you,
whom my heart betrays
and my lips woo.

This is your body
stretched on the cross—
stretched on the world
of profit and loss;

and yet this body
lepered with sores
is holy still
because it is yours;

still is yours
because it gives
grace to the leper:
because it lives.

Jesus crucified
in your Church
all down history;
while we lurch

up ways of sorrow
carry us still,
the heavy cross of us,
up the hill

to Omega
and Easter's height—
your risen body
strong as light.

RAYMOND GARLICK

TERMINAL

A small boy, four years
Or so of age,
And tired and confused,
In a noisy, crowded building,
His ears still hurting
From some mysterious ailment,
He trails behind his parents,
Tired too, if less confused.

Then the people all take sides,
Like in a game,
His father joins the Caucasian file,
His mother the Other.
Which team is his team?
He hears them talking,
His English father, Chinese mother,
And the man who owns the building,

Who rubs his head:
'There's this queue and there's that queue,
There isn't any third queue.
I don't know what to say!'

Neither does the little boy,
He is tired and confused.
In front of him the two queues stretch away,
There isn't any third queue.

D. J. ENRIGHT

THE SENSITIVE PHILANTHROPIST

If I give you money,
Give you baksheesh,
Will you stay away
Until next week?

Since money talks
We don't need to,
Neither you to me
Nor me to you.

If I give you money
Will you make sure
That the others keep away,
Without me giving more?

Will you promise
To put to flight
All your legless colleagues
By day and by night?

If I give you money
Will you agree
To hide your stump away,
Where I can't see?

Will you state in writing
That it was done on purpose
And doesn't really hurt,
The arms, the legs, the nose?

Can't I send a cheque
Regular each week
By registered letter,
So we need never meet?

D. J. ENRIGHT

WITCH HUNT

'Frying tonite'—
The forge is hot
Beat out your steel
There's lots to die tonight

'Frying tonite'—
The coals are hot
Thrust in your tongs
There's flesh to talk tonight

'Frying tonite'—
The oven's hot
Rubber aprons on
They're all lined up tonight

'Frying tonite'—
The fires are hot
Pull on your masks
There's blacks to burn tonight

'Frying tonite'—
The napalm's hot
Press down the switch
And kill us all tonight.

PHILIP PADFIELD

SPY

We who were once so open
    have forgotten how to give
        eat alone
dream our dreams in corners
leave messages unsigned on walls

There is a traitor in our midst
we have been warned he could be
    nearer than we think

Shoulder to shoulder we sit in the room
    eyeing each other
over the tops of newspapers

LINDSAY LEVY

THE KILL

Slowly he is
killing her.
              We
stand round and watch
fascinated
by the dragged breasts
the drops of blood.

Honestly we
would do something
bring cream cakes, sweet
cider, words but
it is too late
she moans *it is*
too late when we
go near.
              Besides
how she lies there!

When she is dead
we will put on
fine clothes and walk
behind him in
the procession
bearing candles
and ringing bells.

KEITH BOSLEY

FREEDOM
(Holloway, Spring 1969)

Here at least, I thought,
I shall find freedom.
Here in prison all encumbrances
will be removed.
I shall be left without the burden of
possessions, responsibilities, relationships.
Alone and naked I shall feel
a fresh wind over my entire uncluttered body
blow each pore clear,
cooling and cleaning every crevice.

At last I shall know the relief of
simply obeying orders,
owning nothing,
caring for no-one,
being uncared for.

I shall sit content for hours on end
in a bare cell,
glad to be cut off from
things, people, commitments and the
confusing world outside.

But I was wrong.
There is no freedom here—
prison is the world in microcosm.

In my locker is a cache of valuables:
needle, cotton, nail-file, pencil.
My wages buy me fruit and biscuits which
I hoard and hide,
fearing they'll get stolen.

Meticulously I arrange the flowers that
outside friends send in;
carefully decorate my cell with cut out pictures;
get flustered if I lose my mug or bucket.

I am no hermit from the outside world,
but strain through busy days to read
each item in the newspapers.
International problems follow me inside;
a prisoner is picked on—she is coloured.

Every evening I am forced to choose
between a range of recreations:
I may read or dance or take a bath,
go to class, play darts or
watch the news.

I am seldom on my own:
a geometry of love, hate, friendship
forms about me.
Someone calls my name,
enters my cell,
asks a favour,
makes some claim upon me.

And I marvel
as I lie alone at night
that this world is as complex as the other;
that even here in jail I am not free to
lose my freedom.

    PAT ARROWSMITH

GONE MAD

A world gone mad.
Is it a world gone mad?
But still the swallows bring the summer back.
Chatter and peck and beak and claw
Fly, fly a thousand times
But cast some of the weakest from the nest,
A bird can do so much, only so much.
Chatter and peck and beak and claw
And guard the little hell against all comers.
Thus the swallows bring the summer back
Into a world gone mad.

PATRICIA DOUBELL

NATIONAL SERVICE

Give me a wind thick
  With useless leaves
And I will salute it.
  Let me hear the sun slink
At tea time, and I will
  Stand to attention.
If the soil trembles for fear
  Of frost, I will lie
On my face, with my legs apart.
  In this red season my
Blood is khaki-coloured and my spine
  Shivers for the whisper of orders.

MICHAEL STEVENS

SANG FIR EWAN (MA SON).

Six months and ye try wards,   (words)
Bit nae wards come,   (no)
   ma peerie doo. (a term of endearment)
Six months and at nicht   (night)
Ye gurgle awa dreams,
   ma peerie doo.

Six months and smiles
Mak ma hert loup,   (heart; leap)
   ma peerie doo.

And whit's tae come,   (what's)
I ken nocht,   (nothing)
   ma peerie doo.

Bit gin ye haud tae Love,   (if; hold)
   ma peerie doo,
Gin ye haud tae Truth,
   ma peerie doo,
Gin ye strive fir Peace,   (for)
   ma peerie doo,

Ye s'all haud tae a guid Trinitie; (good)
Ye s'all haud tae Life,
   ma peerie doo.

Six months, and I ken nocht
o whit's tae come.
I fear fir whit's tae come,
   ma peerie, peerie doo.

DAVID MORRISON

FIRE AT THE WAR MUSEUM
Formerly BEDLAM

As always merely dozing
the wily old heartbreaker
   roused from his tomb by a petrol bomb
cavorts through lousy acre

perennial king of bedlam
with his angry steel-forged member.
   His subjects? Bones of your perfect sons
who'll respect him come november.

His crown biliously corroded
can still bring tourists gazing:
   who'd not admire this dome of fire
with its bloody splinters blazing?

His butch boys itch for action
as each poxy cannon thunders
   where the flame leaves play screams ricochet
from incarcerated blunders.

Since careless meths-high jesters
let lovers seige his borders
   (scabbed plane trees yield in bedlam's field
sly shade for petting marauders)

Who needs evoke this spectre
that rides with charred claws reeking?
   Beware I say what's begun today
may provoke scars no man's seeking.

Dance you audacious couples
arabesques more bold than hoses
  lay the crazy ghosts of these gaunt hosts—
with kind kisses weave them roses

PETER ROBINS

'TO CHILDREN ARDENT FOR SOME DESPERATE GLORY'

(WILFRED OWEN)

Lucky are the Viet Cong,
They can do nothing wrong.
They are only bombed,
They cannot bomb;
Only they are napalmed,
They don't, can't, napalm.
All the mass atrocities
Are on one side; idealism,
Courage, are on theirs.
If they were ten times as strong,
We'd see war as it really is
Freed from partial images.
Nor is Che Guevara in the jungle
With six friends, typical
Of H Bombs and state armies.
Idealists, rapt in theories,
Must sense that world war means
Their side burning babies,
Before their ardent dreams
Drift to earth as dust, germs, gases.

NORMAN ILES

BACK TO THE DRAWING-BOARD

It was nice lying under the trees to think they might still
    be there for our coming children,
it was nice to think our children might be born,
it would have been nice.
Now all our possibilities have resolved inevitably into
    sterile dust
and our ashes settling after the fireball, perhaps one day
the odd viruses that survived will start again, perhaps one day
there will be new lovers under new trees breathing new
    wishes for their coming children,
and perhaps, next time, again, they'll be ignored.

GEOFF BARNBROOK

BUT MURDEROUS

A Mother slew her unborn babe
In a date of recent date
Because she did not wish him to be born in a world
Of murder and war and hate
'Oh why should I bear a babe from my womb
To be broken in pieces by a hydrogen bomb?'

I say this woman deserves little pity
That she was a fool and a murderess
Is a child's destiny to be contained by a mind
That signals only a lady in distress?

And why should human infancy be so superior
As to be too good to be born in this world?
Did she think it was an angel or a baa-lamb
That lay in her belly furled?

Oh the child is the young of its species
Alike with that noble, vile, curious and fierce
How foolish this poor mother to suppose
Her act told us aught that was not murderous

(As, item, That the arrogance of a half-baked mind
Breeds murder; makes us all unkind.)

STEVIE SMITH

THE WORLD TOMORROW

We share a common grief,
Lucky or unlucky ones:
The burnt-out leaf,
The flash brighter than a thousand suns.
Where are we going, where
Into what future terrors,
While the loaded air
Holds our past errors?
Or that dark way refuse:
The world healed, wise
And beautiful, choose
For our children's eyes?

DOUGLAS GIBSON

FOUR

SONG

Proud old woman plays guitar,
Her voice they say is coloured,
Though we must listen from afar,
Some things apartheid cannot bar,
What colour sings the blackbird?
Proud old woman with guitar,
Your voice is multi-coloured.

Frightened man without a song,
He whistles in the darkness,
The road is narrow, road is long,
He hides his conscience in the throng,
But he can still tell right from wrong,
Frightened man, you hear the song,
It's whistling in the darkness.

A mob is made of ones and twos,
Its strength is in its numbers,
Yours is the name that they must use,
You are the one who's in the news,
If you say no then they will lose
For protests come by ones and twos,
Their strength is in their numbers.

KEN WLASCHIN

COLOUR

Red, black, white or yellow,
What does it matter?
If you work,
You are my brother.

J. H. THOMAS

MAN MAKES HIMSELF

(in memory of Friedrich Engels and Gordon Childe)

The ape-man grips a clumsy axe
And ushers in the man.
But when he's cracked a bone with it
He lets it drop as done.

After five hundred thousand years
He chips the double edge
And stares at the advancing ice
Under his forehead ridge.

Soon he will think before he moves
And feel before he speaks
And cutting with the single edge
Discuss before he makes.

Soon he will eat the souls of bears,
Want what he cannot have,
And paint a bird he never saw
On the wall of a hidden cave.

Because of these two million years
The man is housed and shod
And upright (in the physical sense)
But still he dreams of gods.

Now he racks himself between
The body and the soul
And will not trust his mastery
Of language and of tool.

His eyes turn inwards more than out,
Look up and sigh for more,
And while his body rests, a soul
Creeps in at the back door.

How many generations more
Before our kingdom comes
And, dying and living for this world,
We make ourselves at home?

DAVID CRAIG

WHAT A CENTURY

Tunnelling in the caves of sky
The aero-engines dirl round and round
As though the whole universe were crying
Drearily for mankind.

Even a train
Clinking its wagons on familiar tracks
Brings back those generations of pain—
People herded to death in battened trucks.

What a century.
Every image hides a perverted symbol.
Everything we make
Can be a tool for the shambles.

Only a generation of use,
Lifting the hand to work and not to wound,
Could grow new tissue in the scarred mind
And heal the long abuse.

DAVID CRAIG

SILLYSUIT

This is a sillysuit I wear
an elbow through
the seat threadbare
and I don't know where
I'll wear it
again.

I wore it to the Palace
when they told me that the Queen
was hiding in the ivy
somewhere inbetween
the East Wing & the West Wing.

I wore it to the Castle
when they handed out the arms
and I heard the choristers
singing the psalms—
up to their thighs in ammunition.

I wore it to the Chapel
where the men were on their knees
praying to whatever gods
and all saying please—
as blue as their eyes the salvation.

    I wore it to the brewery
    I wore it to the fair
    I wore it to make love in
    & I wore it everywhere.

So Stitch & Snippit tailorman
cut another suit
sew it in the latest style
and let the trumpets toot
there is one reveille
I won't answer.

This is a billet-doux I bear
signed by Her Majesty
and that's quite rare
but I don't have a care
to wear that
again.

PETE MORGAN

DOWN BY THE RIVER

Walking through the long grass
on our way to the river,
my son wanders ahead, hunting
imaginary lions, happy
and contented in his game.
The day is closing down,
storm clouds gathering,
and a fresh breeze
ripples across the fields
from the sea.
                    A jet-plane
screams through the air, and
the child comes running,
clutching my hand, and pulling
his hood up as the wind
whips through the grass.
The rain starts to fall,
and as we stand on the river bank
I look at the dark clouds overhead.

JIM BURNS

CAUSE AND EFFECT

He thought before the war
Of conflicts, heroism, enemies
Who had to be crushed;
Causes that had to be fought for.

He had no time before the war
For bright skies, fields, the warm
Sun, his woman—only
Causes that had to be fought for.

I see him now after the war
In my lifetime. I notice his love
Of the sun, bright skies, fields, his woman:
Causes that have to be fought for.

ALAN BOLD

CHARACTER OF THE HAPPY GUERILLA

Sure, I'm for freedom,
Without it, life's not much.
With nothing else,
Freedom's not much either.

If no lines were drawn
Who would stir his stumps?
Boundaries exclude us,
They also invite us.

Vive the small difference
Of this state from that!
Free people die of boredom,
Looking keeps us living.

> The landscape's poxed
> And patched with frontiers.
> Once I was a teacher
> Of literature;
> I failed to perceive
> That the whole of the literature of Europe
>   from Homer
> Composed a simultaneous order.
> I could only see the borders,
> The existing monuments,
> Toll gates, guard houses and gun sites,
> A landscape disordered
> By a thousand simultaneous poets.

Sure, it's a dog's life,
Being hounded:
But every dog has its day.
Keep your boots dubbined,
Sheath-knife sharp, story
In good shape, smart but not fancy.

It's not as if
There's so much competition for it,
For freedom.
There's enough to go round
If you go round looking for it.
It's usually across the border.

D. J. ENRIGHT

MATTERS ARISING

No doubt what you say is right.
In Wales we shall never see
a terrible beauty born.
No rose of tragedy,
petalled in crimson and black,
will sway on this post office roof.
Swansea gaol will receive
no heroes, unshaven, aloof,
for the cells' chill liturgy
and the rites of the firing-squad.
Whatever beauty's in blood
will not bloom here, thank God.

I met an Easter man
in Dublin long ago,
Senator, Minister now,
who told me: 'You will know
when you find yourself picking off,
like roses whose day is done,
from behind a garden wall
the soldiers of Albion—
you'll know as you see them fall,
and you feel the frost of fear
icing your ambushed spine,
that what you hope for is near'.

I have lived where blood
had flooded down men's hands.
Though I look for a Wales
free as the Netherlands,
a freedom hacked out here
is a freedom without worth,
a terror without beauty.
Here it must come to birth
not as a pterodactyl
flailing archaic wings,
but the dove that broods on chaos—
wise as a thousand springs.

RAYMOND GARLICK

APOLOGIA

Your Wales was never mine, I know.
The towering shadows the dead throw
lie like elegies over your day.
I usually face the other way.
For you the present is the last
dying moment of the past.
For me the present is the first
leaf-green bud from which will burst
the future, like an un-named rose
for my children's hands to close
themselves around, bend to and breathe:
the flowering Wales that you bequeath.

RAYMOND GARLICK

THE ABILITY TO. . . .

Lately
I have come to know a voice
like old walls
that have always been there
and I've never realised their crack
                    and cranny beauty.

It seems there is a voice
that creates a space
for love and me to lie in,

a voice that is not quiet
                    not loud
but is as strong as the sun
smashing fire into passing windows.

A voice that has been passed
from one kind dead hand
to a harsh living one

the voice and I
are not particular companions,
we exist together
there are no explanations
but the ability to do and see
O—many things.

DEREK TELLING

BE DAMNED

Be damned if he can
there are things that will take him
and pain will issue out from a man.
The river in full flood
will catch him unaware
will infect his strong blood
and there hardly be time to curse and swear.

Be damned if he can always be gentle
the sights he'll see will take him
and the rage that'll burn him/turn him almost mental,
his tired head and mad eyes
beaten by the sun
lifted to the skies
will care for no-one.

Be damned grey brain
spewing over the edge of the white skull
finally pray for the sanctity that never came
during the sanguine life of the pure revolution,
guns and crosses mark the page
of the great constitution
quicklime to the bones of the original sage.

Be damned cry and sigh
and ask why

the same question lies
sealed in remembrance days
poppy patter of auld lang synes
deep in graveyard ways.

Be damned if he can
as yet, be a peaceful man.

DEREK TELLING

DEMONSTRATOR

I am the dream of bound apprentices
who starved through amber-filtered centuries;
I am the gathered rage of harvesters
muted at twenty under parish rags

I am the boy whose head you cannot bend
in deference, as did his forefathers';
my glance is not confused by patched-up flags—
to me, all gilt-edged frontiers are a joke.

I have inherited a winter world
devoid of sunlight; hungry; derelict
where most are dumb with guilt, except the young
who have not prospered on their brothers' graves.

I, your moment's pleasure, owe you little
whatever your spry hucksters choose to yell;
I, your own green days, rise in the whirlwind
of shattered leaves now beating on your door.

I speak for an emerging generation
questioning all, articulate at last:
it is not years but hope divides us from you—
where there is none, how can mere doors resist?

PETER ROBINS

EDINBURGH RAIN & LOVE POEM

once in Edinburgh
I had a sudden
urge
to post your letter
down a drain

not because
I was tiring of you

but because

my thoughts should reach you
anyhow

through grates
through orange peel
through dirty water

LINDSAY LEVY

DWELLING AMONG SCARRED HILLS

Dwelling among scarred hills
they are not yet born
—those who love the earth:
for their lives are many times past
and their knocking on the door
is yet of the future.

Waiting
they shake cold staring stars
into their closed baskets:
arms reaching
from tormented graves
pluck at the earth
which is but a cancer
of the sky's creation.

Through all their wounds
they are all the soft and beautiful
creatures of the land.

their faces
though never known
are not quite
forgotten

Somewhere
a voice which lives
in peace with itself
waits to whisper
'So you have come
at last'

TINA MORRIS

THE ABSENCES

At such moments
absence dominates:
absence, for example,
of trees for birds
to hang their song upon,
of leaves for snow
to spread its fingers on:
absence of noise,
the restless traffic
finally at peace,
absence of time
as it resumes its unity.
Talk of war and rape,
ministers of state
screaming blinkered hate
across the pages—
all absent. Instead
newspapers talk of
mighty efforts
to save life,
encouraging us
to succour the old,
leave bread
for starving birds.
And they still sell:
survival has suddenly
become of interest.

Waiting in queues
and on platforms
people nod sympathetically
to one another—even joke:
children, kings again,
fortress the streets
with laughter.
Old and young, the sick,
the fit, the rich, the poor,
kneel before one altar.
Snow's white flag of truce
strangles the city's roar.

JEREMY ROBSON

PEACE IS A PERFECT SHELL

Peace is a perfect shell
Lying on the seashore, after a tank landing.
Peace is the family portrait
Intact upon the wall of the bombed house.
Peace is the small community left in the world
After the nuclear war; who greet one another,
Agree to share a cave, build, marry and have children.

So why land the tanks?
Why bomb the house?
Why destroy the world?

For people will always fight to preserve peace,
And peace will always outlive them, untouched.
Peace is a catalyst,
And it is harder to live with it than to die for it.

MARJORIE BALDWIN

A LETTER TO A FEW GOOD POETS I KNOW

Guns are made of steel & wood but the
wondrous giver of life is flesh between your legs.
Your future is ever fused with the beauty without
for it knows no form other than the creating &
making of things & the gentle nourishing of life.
History saw many cruel leaders, vast armies,
slaughtered peoples, much suffering & grim death.
You must each free yourself from leaders,
passports, territories, & all barriers which
seek to divide, & grow as new free men
amongst us; the mad patriot forever destroyed.
You who must warn of the cancer of money & greed,
the politician, mercenary, judge, hangman &
censor; the terrible prophet messenger of death.
You who must embrace the men & women of
love, tolerance & peace; the makers of life.

DAVE CUNLIFFE

& ALL OUR GODS SHALL TREMBLE

He will be the kind of man who has
no need to dream of love or peace.
He will be the sort of guy who
intuitively knows that most special
things of our time & all time
are really just so much useless crap.
Truth shall never sour within his mouth.
Yet how can such a man ever again
appear amid this utter desolation.
His terrible beauty still not for our
troubled eyes whose agony is of the beast.
If & when the day shall come when we
grow tired or bored of these slaughters
& come to dread death as we now fear
life then we may yet be blest enough
to embrace this real human man.
& all our gods shall tremble for
we will have no more need of them.

DAVE CUNLIFFE

EROS AT THE MARKETS

Peach, apple, orange, pear;
Covent Garden porters' prayer:
thick psalms of love.

Pumpkin, onion, celery, bean;
from the earth's convulsed machine
comes broth of love.

Box, basket, carton, crate;
to each the markets allocate
consigned love.

Trailer, trolley, barrow, van;
Long Acre's dusty orchards scan
pastorals of love.

Driver, porter, clerk, youth;
robust replicas of truth:
you, me, love.

LAURENCE COLLINSON

MEDITATION

(with a debt to Krishnamurti)

It's no good seeking peace.
A state that's sought
Is never attained.
There is always the gap
Between you and it.

If you see that you are violence,
Without condemning yourself
For being violence
Or justifying yourself
For being violence,
There is in that perception
Transformation.

JEAN OVERTON FULLER

OLYMPICS

The sweetness was the
Atmosphere. Not merely
The beauty, the perfection,
Of the golden athlete.
The climate was consideration.
Not shown to this extent
At the Olympics before:
Kindness opened like a boy
Smiles. This is the test.
Not the ultra-human effort
Of physical endurance, that
Spell-binder! The hosts
Turning the international
Achievement into national,
One nation, one people. The
Sweetness was the atmosphere.

MADGE HALES

SEPTEMBER SONG

Be not too hard for life is short
And nothing is given to man;
Be not too hard when he is sold and bought
For he must manage as best he can;
Be not too hard when he gladly dies
Defending things he does not own;
Be not too hard when he tells lies,
And if his heart is sometimes like a stone
Be not too hard—for soon he dies,
Often no wiser than he began;
Be not too hard for life is short
And nothing is given to man.

CHRISTOPHER LOGUE

EASTER COMMUNION

(Aldermaston Easter Rally in Hyde Park)

Among the trees and bushes banners swayed,
Skipping with colour, or with captions black
As death; and under them the marshalled pack
Of foot-pricked, side-stitched demi-martyrs stayed
A while on pagan grass; and sang, or played,
Or idled on the ground, or had a snack,
As from the altar-rostrum to the back
Of a great nave host upon host was laid.

Could anyone there by chance ever hope to find
A common inspiration—what hopes, fears,
What prayers or rational debate to give;
Tokens of world brotherhood, purblind
Unreasonings—yes, crankiness and tears—
Rich creeds or simple words, 'I want to live'.

DAVID TRIBE

LET US GIVE THANKS

let us give thanks to the love that made us,
and the hare and the tree
and the white moor,
and to the bird and the stone let us sing.
let us shake the branches that are laden;
with snow let us blanket the world
and lock with frost the rain and the river,
the clouds the hills and the night.
let us run in the wind and listen to sky-works
in the sand of our voices.
let us be one with the eye of the sun
glittering across the blue pool of heaven,
striking white onto white in the drifts
and icicles of light.
let us dance at the top of the world, you and I,
together let us sing of the stillness:
come,
my hand is ready . . . .

TREVOR LAWRENCE

THE LONG WALK

On the long walk
From Aldermaston to London
I saw a stranger
Walking with a limp,
Dragging a blistered foot.

He sat aside to rest.
But when I went to help
The man beside me said,
'He is a Russian'. In
Such a tone of voice.

He is a spy. He is
A dirty dog. He is
Not one of us. Even
His blister is a
Fiendish subterfuge.

His blister was most real.
So was his gratitude.
Pain knows no language bar;
Plasters no politics.
Smiling, we journeyed on.

But not two strangers.
Just two weary men
Going the same way
For the same reason
On the long walk.

BILL PICKARD

FOLK SONG

Would you like to take a freedom walk
When some don't care and the others mock
And it's safer to sit at home and talk
Than build the Freedom Rock.

Do you want to march for freedom now
Or wait ten years till they tell you how
You've got to do more than they'll allow
To sing the Freedom Rock.

Are you scared to make that freedom run
When someone out there is holding a gun
And for all you know you may be the one
Shot on the Freedom Rock.

Black and white and yellow and red
There's equal freedom when you're dead
But some of us want it for the living instead
Upon the Freedom Rock.

We'll all be together on the final march
And there's no turning back when the road gets harsh
For this time there can't be a next time farce
Or there'll be no Freedom Rock.

KEN WLASCHIN

LIVING

Unless a corn of wheat
Falls into the ground and dies
It lives alone.

Dying is mostly painful,
Unless one is sure
Of a resurrection.

That is why there are
So many bachelors,
Mostly married.
So few husbands.

By the same token,
So many career girls,
Married or single.
So few wives.

For children
The choice is delayed,
But soon, too soon,
The choice must be made.

To live alone alone,
To live alone
With somebody,
Or to live.

BILL PICKARD

TO THE POETS OF THE SEVENTIES

we are the children
coming into our own
turning from the old ways
to a decade of possibilities
flower. harp. nuclear fire.
pyramid. the edges run

so small and weak they are
so preciously tender in
our hands that they
will run like sand through
the fingers hold them close
or they will slide away

our hands may shake
but the fist is grown huge
the braincomb multiplied
and no different in essence
no less pitiless to wield
the thunderbolt over the
cabins of the poor over
the barren lands

and on the rim of a vortex:
who would look at the stars?
except the fortunate ones
except maybe the survivors
the tree in my ear is scorched
with concepts the masks
have blinded me let us make
a new thing for ourselves
let us stand watch
over the coming years

ROBERT CONRAD

Acknowledgements

Acknowledgements are made to the following publishers for permission to reprint:

Chatto and Windus Ltd	Alan Bold's CAUSE AND EFFECT and ON SEEING VOSKHOD OVER EDINBURGH (To Find The New)
Hogarth Press Ltd	Laurie Lee's THE LONG WAR (Selected Poems)
Longman Group Ltd	Stevie Smith's THE PHOTOGRAPH and BUT MURDEROUS (The Frog Prince)
Macmillan & Co Ltd	Keith Bosley's THE KILL and PIETÀ (The Possibility of Angels)

The following poems have also been published previously:

FREEDOM and PRISON DRAWING by Pat Arrowsmith, in 'Twentieth Century'
GREENHOUSE by Pat Arrowsmith, in 'Tribune'
INNOCENT'S SONG and FOR AN EX-FAR EAST PRISONER OF WAR by Charles Causley, in 'Johnny Alleluia' (Hart-Davis)
DEFINITION and THE LOVER ON RETURNING FROM THE WARS by Laurence Collinson, 'The Moods Of Love' (Overland, Australia)
BRIEFING FOR TROPIC WAR by Bruton Connors, in 'Breakthru' and 'Twentieth Century'
A PINT BEFORE CLOSING TIME by Bruton Connors, in 'Poetry Wales'
EVENT by James Corbett, in 'Young Commonwealth Poets 1965' (Heinemann)
MEDALS by James Corbett, in 'Meanjin Quarterly'
NEWS OF A DISTANT WAR by James Corbett, in 'Workshop'
THE DEATH OF THE NUCLEUS by David Craig, in 'New Saltire'
THE RUNAWAY HEART by Patricia Doubell, in 'Workshop'
CHARACTER OF THE HAPPY GUERILLA and THE SENSITIVE PHILANTHROPIST by D. J. Enright, in 'The Listener'
TERMINUS by D. J. Enright, in 'The New Statesman'
APOLOGIA, MATTERS ARISING and PASSION 67 by Raymond Garlick, in 'Collected Poems 1954–1968' (Gwas Gower)
THE WORLD TOMORROW by Douglas Gibson, in 'The New York Times'
THE LAST ONE by Madge Hales, in 'The Listener'
TRAMP IN A WELFARE STATE by Paul Hart, in 'Cyclops'
COFFEE ON THE BALCONY by Pete Hoida, in 'The Empty Flagpole' (Link Paper Books) and 'Cyclops'
GOING FOR A SONG by Geoffrey Holloway, in 'The London Magazine'
DEMOLITION by Norman Iles, in 'Breakthru'
HORSES IN A FIELD by Michael Johnson, in 'For My Rat' (Outposts Publications) and 'The Poet'
I SAW A MAN WITH POPPIES by Michael Johnson, in 'Tribune'
POLITICAL PRISONER by Michael Johnson, in 'For My Rat'
CAPTAIN LEONARD FEATHER and SILLYSUIT by Pete Morgan, in 'A Big Hat Or What?' (Kevin Press)

'YES,' I SAID, 'BUT IS IT ART?' by Pete Morgan, in 'Akros' and 'Imprint'
ONE FOR SORROW by Philip Padfield, in 'Breakthru'
LIVING by Bill Pickard, in 'Hardware and Software' (Outposts Publications)
A POEM FOR CHRISTOPHER by Vera Rich, in 'Portents and Images' (Mitre Press)
DEMONSTRATOR and I TOO AM CAIN by Peter Robins, in 'A Coexisting Heart' (Mitre Press)
FIRE AT THE WAR MUSEUM by Peter Robins, in 'Peace News'
ANOTHER PLACE and SEEN AGAIN by Jeremy Robson, in 'In Focus' (Allison & Busby)
THE ABSENCES by Jeremy Robson, in 'Thirty Three Poems' (Sidgwick & Jackson)
ANGEL BOLEY by Stevie Smith, in 'The New Statesman'
THE ABILITY TO . . . by Derek Telling, in 'Asylum Anthology'
TEACHERS and COLOUR by J. H. Thomas, in 'Breakthru'

Copyright

CONTENTS

ONE

TWO

THREE

ALSO
PUBLISHED BY CORGI BOOKS

LOVE, LOVE, LOVE
The New Love Poetry
Edited with an Introduction
by PETE ROCHE
552 07789 5   30p

C'MON EVERYBODY
An anthology of poems on the theme 'Poetry of
the Dance'.
Edited with an introduction by Pete Morgan
552 08571 5   30p

CORGI MODERN POETS IN FOCUS 1-4
The four latest volumes in this series which
feature six different poets in each, their poems
(some of which have not been published previously
in book form) and an introduction to the poet's
work by the editor.
Corgi Modern Poets in Focus 1 and 3
Edited by Dannie Abse
Corgi Modern Poets in Focus 2 and 4
Edited by Jeremy Robson

0 552 { 08766 1   08806 4 } 30p each
       { 08787 4   08144 7 }

THE YOUNG BRITISH POETS
An anthology of work by the younger poets who have
emerged in Britain over the past few years.
Edited by Jeremy Robson
552 08975 3   30p

PUBLISHED BY BANTAM BOOKS

THE POETRY OF ROCK
Edited by Richard Goldstein
552 63964 8   35p

ROCK AND OTHER FOUR LETTER WORDS
J. Marks
552 64334 3   50p

NEW TREASURY OF FOLK SONGS
Tom Glazer
552 64289 4   25p

FOLK SONGS OF THE WORLD
Edited by Charles Haywood
552 63565 0   42½p

THE WORLD'S LOVE POETRY
Edited by Michael Rheta Martin
552 63822 6   50p

All these books are available at your bookshop or newsagent: or can be ordered direct from the publisher. Just tick the titles you want and fill in the form below.

....

CORGI AND BANTAM BOOKS, Cash Sales Department, P.O. Box 11, Falmouth, Cornwall.
Please send cheque or postal order. No currency, and allow 6p per book to cover the cost of postage and packing in U.K., and overseas.

NAME ....

ADDRESS...

(Aug. 72)   ....